BOTTOM OF THE FOOD CHAIN

Bottom of the Food Chain: A Fresh Perspective on How Your Career Impact Goes Beyond Your Job Title by LaPora Lindsey

Published by LaPora Lindsey & Company, LLC.
Colts Neck, New Jersey

www.laporalindsey.com

Editor: Brunella Costagliola at The Military Editor Agency

Cover and Interior Design: Dee the Creative

Illustrator: Kristen Ritter

A special thanks to John Niland of Self-Worth Academy for his permissions to use quotes from his book, "Self-Worth Safari: Valuing Your Life and Your Work."

ISBN: 979-8-9861421-0-4 (Color print)
979-8-9861421-2-8 (B&W print)
ISBN: 979-8-9861421-1-1(ebook)

Printed in the United States

Library of Congress Control Number: 2022914756

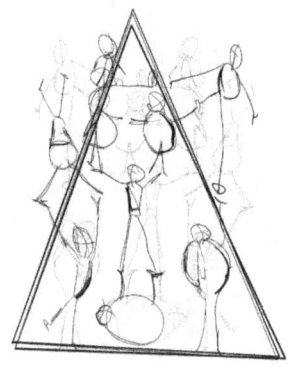

Dedication

This book is dedicated to every person
who has felt inadequacy and believed that
your job or role wasn't enough.
Your role is important.

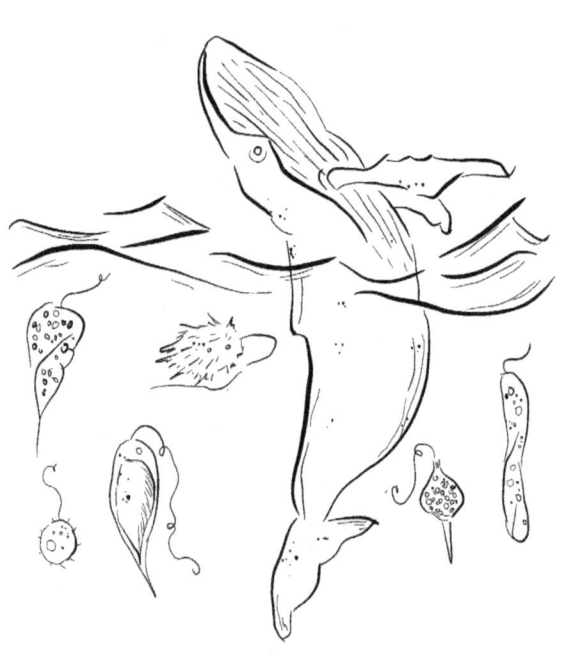

CONTENTS

INTRODUCTION

CHAPTER ONE
POWER IS DOWN   1

CHAPTER TWO
YOU ARE A POWER PRODUCER   15

CHAPTER THREE
ECOSYSTEMS OF IMPACT   29

CHAPTER FOUR
SUSTAINABILTY   39

CHAPTER FIVE
GROWING PAINS   59

CHAPTER SIX
CONTRIBUTION   79

CHAPTER SEVEN
OBSTACLES & POTENTIAL   95

CHAPTER EIGHT
EMBRACE FOR IMPACT   111

ACKNOWLEDGEMENTS

ABOUT THE AUTHOR

INTRODUCTION

It is time to get rid of the negative thoughts that prevent you from growing and blossoming in life, and I have just what it takes for you to acknowledge and embrace your worth finally. The first step is to deconstruct the way society has told you how to estimate and value your worth, but I need your help to do so. I want you to take a pen and paper and draw a triangle. Seriously, go ahead. I'll wait.

Now that you have a beautifully drawn triangle, it's time to label it: The Food Chain. We will call the top of the triangle: *Top*. Original, I know. And let's mark the bottom—wait for it—*Bottom*. Bet you didn't see that one coming. Also listed in this last level is the word, *Photosynthesis*. This is probably giving you science class vibes, isn't it? Don't worry, I won't make you take a quiz when we are done. Once your triangle is complete, it may look like this:

This may look familiar. This is a basic structure of the

THE FOOD CHAIN

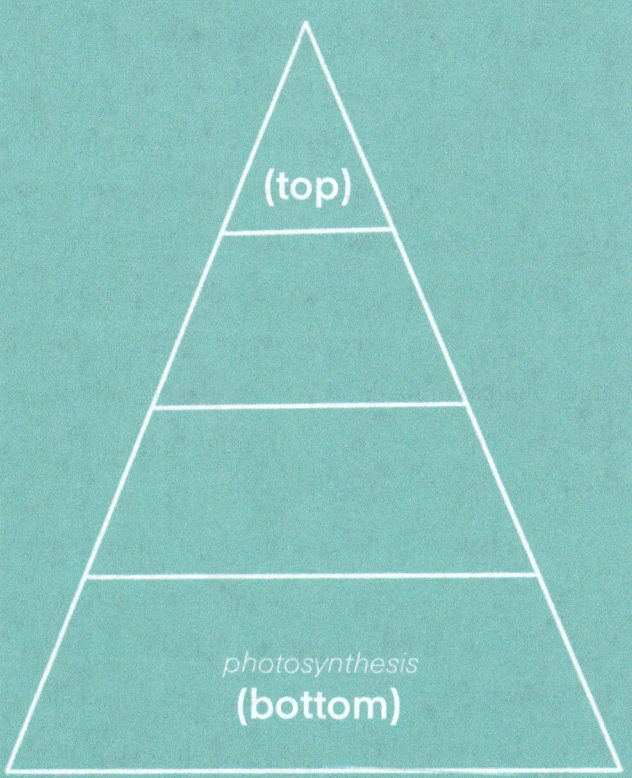

food chain energy pyramid. Take a moment to acknowledge the design and the placement of the words. Notice the two levels between the bottom and the top, which is purposefully left blank (for now). This is the first step to deconstructing the meaning of your self-worth. I have heard "the bottom of the food chain" used as a phrase to refer to the lower portion of a hierarchy in social or work settings. The term has negative connotations, and no one wants to be there. Some well-known references of animals at the top of the food chain are lions, tigers, and (polar) bears—oh, and great white sharks. And at the bottom of the food chain, you will find plants such as grasses, moss, ferns, and underwater plant-like life, such as algae and phytoplankton. At first glance, the bottom of the food chain doesn't look like much, does it? But in just a moment, you will see how it can be.

The bottom is the base in the pyramid, and the foundation produces balance through the amount of energy available. It's the stabilizer. Plants keep things going, growing, and moving. When one animal eats another, the process starts at the bottom when plants create their energy through photosynthesis, and then an animal eats it. This starts the process of transferring energy from one organism to the next, and I think we can all agree that this is a *huge* responsibility for being at the bottom.

As an Educator and Career Coach, I have spent over thirteen years working in higher education, non-profit, and military settings to help people take control of the negative mindset and steer toward the realization that success doesn't need to come with a piece of paper— be it in the form of a title, check, or degree, you don't need it to solidify your worth. Throughout my career, I have seen firsthand how actions at the ground level better the entire organizational structure. I have seen a non-supervisory employee advocate for change within a company that prompted the institution to change its policies and procedures in how they care for patients, making a difference in many people's lives. I have seen people with no diplomas or college degrees create and implement ideas that provided life-changing assistance to others struggling in poverty. Through it all, I have developed an understanding and appreciation for self-worth. It is understanding that I and you, have something to offer. Something uniquely different and regardless of what I or you look like compared to others, regardless of your degree, irrespective of your experience, none of it reflects your self-worth. Self-worth is something that can only come from inside, a measure that only you can decide.

I invite you to look at the food chain with different eyes and appreciate the fact that real sustainability, power, and hope for everlasting and positive change can start right at the bottom—the great white shark would not exist without algae, phytoplankton, or other organisms that are at the bottom of the food chain. Understanding and reevaluating the pyramid related to your achievements are the steps we will cover in this book. My goal is to help you realize that you are a lot closer to creating impact and succeeding than you realize.

The food chain and photosynthesis are scientific terminologies. But also, from religious beliefs to anthropology and other sciences, the connection between humans and plants has long been studied. Amongst those studies, there is a small portion devoted to the relationship between humans and the environment, specifically plants. In the field of horticulture—the art of plant cultivation in gardens for food or ornamental purposes, it expresses the idea that our involvement with plants not only provides us with insights into their meaning, which normally goes unnoticed, but it also provides insights into ourselves. Other theories take this one step further and express that the people-plant interaction can potentially transform how we see ourselves. Based on my view of plants tied into my personal experience, I have seen the power in observing what we are capable of through plant life, and even more so through the food chain. I want to share with you an understanding of plants and how they work to establish a revolutionary and practical awareness that the bottom is not always what it seems.

Throughout this book, we will use the analogy of plant life to discuss general principles of science that can be seen in your work life, but keep in mind that there's one critical difference between the plants and humans, and that will be shared in a later chapter.

The bottom of anything has a purpose, but sometimes we need to change our perspective to see and appreciate its value. This is what this book aims to do: provide you with a guide to increase your self-confidence by turning the meaning of "Worth" upside down. We are constantly bombarded by reminders that we need to keep up. That friend's social media post reminds you that you must keep up with her fitness routine. Your colleague's promotion reminds you that you have to keep up with his work ethic. That magazine cover reminds you that you must keep up with healthier food choices. A never-ending *Be More*, *Do More*.

Just like plants are not required to be at the top of the food chain to be invaluable, success doesn't require a high-profile position for you to see what you are worth. You *are* successful, even if you have never been a leader, never been promoted, or earned over a certain amount of money. Status does not determine your limit. There are many pathways to success and becoming the best version of yourself; both require work, but they also need *you*. The foundational level in the food chain is the stabilizer, and that is where the power lies. If you are at the bottom of the food chain, there is much work to be done, but it is the perfect place to begin the journey to success.

Starting right now.

THE FOOD CHAIN

CHAPTER ONE
POWER IS DOWN

A triangle is about to change your life. More specifically, the energy pyramid and food chain that you have come to know in the introduction. Indeed, this shape will serve as our source of inspiration and reference throughout this book, and it will help you reevaluate your worth.

But you may be wondering: How will this pyramid help me do that? Here's how: This pyramid is a basic representation of the structure of life.

The idea of plants as a symbolism for humans has been around for a while. There have been many analogies, stories, and religions that have referred to the growth of a plant as a symbol of the change in our lives. Additionally, many companies and organizations refer to their services as "Ecosystems." However, one element has not yet been explored: the human connection or metaphor focused on the people at the bottom of that food chain.

THE FOOD CHAIN

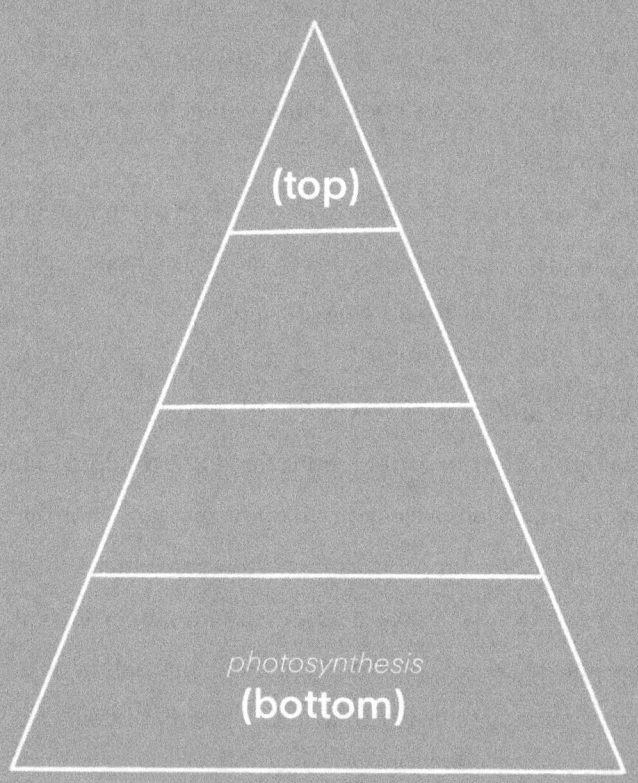

The Food Chain

When you take a closer look at the food chain, you will see that some are on top—in the animal world, this would be referred to as the king of the jungle. In our daily lives, these individuals are admired based on their position, lifestyle, and influence. This could be a person in a high-visibility role, someone with star power, or both. Perhaps they have more money, more praise, and more promotions than most. Someone like an Executive Director or CEO—they are respected by many because of their position and the weight that it holds. They are the leaders of their organizations or companies with levels of individuals reporting up to them, either directly or indirectly, and thus are on the top.

And then some are at the bottom—for most people, this is not where they'd like to be. In the animal world, the plant kingdom rules the bottom as they are rulers over no one, but providers to many. As human beings, these can be individuals who may have worked just as hard as those on the top. Yet, they may earn less money, have a lower position, fewer awards, and less visibility. These individuals can also be considered those in the customer facing roles. In the different settings I have worked in, consistently some of the most notewor-thy coworkers, who could be identified as at the bottom of the food chain, are receptionists. They multi-task as they handle the phones, schedule appointments, answer inquiries, and skillfully craft mental assessments to determine how to best help clients and staff, who at times may be unkind or dismissive to their efforts. And knowing many days that the receptionists were facing struggles in their personal lives and unable to step away from their professional lives, they still took control of their environment. And when they did, they generated a greeting that conveyed such joy and importance that it created a ripple effect of positivity so intense that clients' and customers' overall experience was changed for the better.

That power is one that many of us see and experience, and yet we rarely acknowledge it—until it is lacking. But acknowledgment or no acknowledgment, this example demonstrates the influential power at the lowest level, where a greeting can influence the per-ception of an organization to the point of a positive or negative review. And because of that type of influence, there is a need to understand how this impact can be made without being at the top, which is why the bottom of the pyramid is our focus.

There is significance at the bottom, by understanding that you can start to reassess your worth. Every job, person in the family, and role in social settings is critical, worthy, and has the potential to be successful. So, if you feel that you need to climb to the top of your career ladder or somehow work your way up the career lattice to be worthy and to prove everyone wrong, this pyramid will help you realize that you don't need to do that. You don't need to be more to increase your worth.

Society often celebrates achievement by rewarding us with awards and titles that are framed as victories. And while we may get a sense of accomplishment from these awards, we may also start to define ourselves by those achievements. The more we participate in this process, the more our self-perceptions of competency become a dominant part of our identity. We begin to base our self-worth on our ability to achieve things, whether it's acing tests, getting promoted or getting more things done.

I read two studies conducted on college students and sports or academic achievement. The results revealed that the pressure of measuring worth based on competency, resulted in a more negative outcome, as students were constantly chasing after the goals of being the best. However, students who did not see the pressure in doing well, but instead were focused on their internal value, benefited. This is only one of the many examples of how recognizing self-worth and using it can affect our lives for the better.

Growing up, I remember learning that the pyramid is one of the strongest shapes. The strength of the pyramid comes from its foundation, which is larger than the point at the top. An energy pyramid is often used to describe nature's process of the food chain, where energy is transferred as one thing eats another. And though you may also find the term "food web" as the phrase to describe this chain, one thing is consistent: there are many organisms at the bottom that transfer energy to a smaller number of animals at the top, this also results in each level maintaining less energy transferred, but nevertheless, there is energy present. There are more algae, phytoplankton, trees, and grasses than crocodiles, lions, and leopards. For the food chain to operate properly, the bottom of the chain must remain at the most substantial level, in numbers and usefulness.

At the lowest level, plants or plant-like organisms obtain light from the sun and convert it into energy for nutrients and growth. That process is called photosynthesis, and this is where the initial power in the food chain originates. At the bottom, to exist requires hard work. While work is being done to create and maintain self-existence, others are depleting the sustenance for their survival, and this is true for the animal world and in our lives as people. Based on *this* information, the bottom is not the desired place to be.

I can recall countless movies, shows, songs, and even daily conversations that provided a negative connotation of the bottom of the food chain. When I worked as a volunteer receptionist, I had customers give me unsolicited advice that I could work my way up if I worked hard enough. When I worked as a retail associate, I had coworkers suggest that I was too good to perform in the job I had. While unintended, both of those occurrences resulted in me feeling like I had not yet succeeded. Even though I had dedicated time and effort to be employed (unpaid and paid) in both of those roles, it still wasn't enough to be considered as successful or as being on top.

As a result of those conversations and many other experiences, I felt that for me to reach my potential, I needed to work my way up because no one ever recommended working to stay at the lowest level to succeed—but you and I are going to explore a different perspective about the base level, because there is power at the bottom.

One common example of the bottom of the food chain is grass. Grass is located at the bottom of the food chain, and it comes in different types, heights, densities, and shades. In many aspects, aside from its possible aesthetic appeal, grass may be viewed as useless or as a chore. Grass goes through photosynthesis, transforming light into energy and nutrients. Then one day along comes a grasshopper who eats a blade of grass here and there and garners nutrients from it. Not long after the grasshopper has eaten its meal, it then becomes a meal. A mouse nibbles up the grasshopper. As that mouse consumes the grasshopper, the mouse also consumes the nutrients that the grasshopper consumes from the grass. The next day, a snake slithers, traps, and then eats the mouse. Moving one mandible at a time, the snake obtains nutrition from the mouse. Through ingestion of the mouse, the snake also receives the nutrients from the grasshopper who ate the grass. After the snake has concluded its meal, a hawk scoops up the snake for dinner—unfortunately for the snake, it's not a date. Once again, as the hawk eats the snake, the nutrients and energy are transferred from one animal to another. Throughout this entire process, the power from the grass at the bottom of the food chain was able to have a beneficial impact on all the animals in the chain, thus proving that there is purpose and power at the bottom. Let's take a note from the grass regarding our potential.

Anything at the bottom has intention, purpose, and meaning. So, if you feel you are at the bottom, remember that your worth can potentially impact many other lives for the better, just like grass. The key is being authentic with yourself to find your value and share it. Grass doesn't try to work its way up the food chain, so there is no challenge of being authentic, it just is—unless it's fake grass, but that's for another time.

As humans, we see what the bottom looks like and what the top looks like. The top can look more appealing for several reasons, but I hope that you can appreciate that every blade of grass is amazing and beneficial, and it just so happens to be a part of the foundational basis of the pyramid. The bottom attains and contributes to success, and you can increase your worth there. Keep in mind that increasing your value may or may not result in an increase in status but take comfort in knowing that you do not need to increase in status to be successful! There are multiple ways to succeed.

My Dad in the Food Chain

My father served in the military, and there is one story he often shares that has stayed with me. This story has helped me to understand self-worth. My father worked on military aircrafts, and as he will tell you, he was at the bottom. Whatever people told him to do, he did it. On top of that, it was the 1970s, and as a Black man in an all-White division, he still had many other obstacles to face. A challenge arose when a helicopter had a faulty "Fire Detection" alarm. The light that would constantly light up whenever the aircraft was turned on. Even after having the aircraft sent over to the offi-cer-in-charge at the Maintenance Department, no one was able to locate where the issue was coming from. The problem made its way up the chain, only to come back down the chain, to my father. He was not the designated person to resolve the issue, nevertheless, he was entrusted with the responsibility because he had previously made comments about other projects that resulted in a positive solution. As he walked around the helicopter, his coworkers commented that he was ill-equipped to find the problem. He was the lowest ranking and so his skills and what he had to offer should inherently be less—or so they thought. He ignored them as he circled the aircraft a total of seven times before he eventually stood in front of the helicopter. He lifted the hood and within seconds he located the battery compartment. Inside, he found two cable cords rubbing each other— the problem. The aircraft was soon fixed and ready to fly. Remember, he was at the bottom of the food chain, and he was not moving up that chain any time soon; but none of that mattered when it came time to demonstrate his value. My father knew he had something valuable to offer and after years of improving his skills, increasing his knowledge, and bettering himself, he had the oppor- tunity to hone in on his true potential and show his value to support the command mission. Time and time again, he was entrusted with solving issues that could have had significant adverse consequences and he continued to solidify his worth. It did not increase his status; he did not move up the food chain. He was not promoted. He did not receive a raise. But does that make him any less successful? I think not. He demonstrated his worth, with or without the accolades. You may have similar stories where you have contributed and impacted someone else's life. Whether you have seen the end result or not, your value and your actions make a difference.

Reflection

Now that I have shared with you the power at the bottom of the food chain, take some time and reflect on your experiences. Try to write down at least one example where you were able to make an impact. You don't have to be extremely detailed, but it's important to acknowledge that your actions matter. Here is some space for you to recognize and write your significance. Here are some additional questions to ask yourself:

1. How does my work affect the company or organization that I am a part of?

2. What would happen to the company if no one did my job?

CHAPTER TWO
YOU ARE A POWER PRODUCER

Around fourteen years ago I was unable to impress my then supervisor. During that time, I was consistently reprimanded for not taking initiative on projects and presentations and there had been a string of work parties each weekend that included everyone except for me. I dreaded going to work each morning, but at the same time, I felt I had something to prove. I needed to make it work, both professionally and socially. I was still a graduate student and needed a job to keep paying for my education. I needed to show that I was worthy.

A few months later, after consistent effort, after yet being unable to demonstrate that I was worthy of my supervisor's standards socially or professionally, I was let go from that job. The feeling of inadequacy overwhelmed me, and I cried for days. I spent years afterward toiling with the idea that I failed. I was chasing after success and missed it. And then I tried and missed it again, and again. At that time for me success meant upward progression only, so there was much frustration as I sat at the bottom. I did not have a desire to be there, and no one could tell me otherwise. I remember being in that spot, sitting at the bottom, yet looking up to see the top. I felt intimidated in the presence of others who had succeeded. My inability to succeed through the ranks caused me to feel inferior. Seeing others have the job that I felt I deserved, the salary that I wanted, and the appearance that I desired—it hurt. And no matter how hard I worked, I couldn't get there.

Is this a familiar story? Feeling stuck is painful. It's a real emotion that resides in your body and one you might experience far too often if you don't take any action to change it.

So indeed, I was at the bottom of the food chain, but I had an influential power that I didn't realize existed–my self-worth. But had you asked me back then I would have told you that I needed the money and the position to make a difference. There was potential for me to pursue change within that organizational structure, but I didn't see the opportunity in me to do that at the time. I was not aware that to be influential and share my worth with others I needed to first recognize or identify what I had to offer. Years later, I continued to try and prove myself to others and increase the value in how others saw me—but most of the time it left me feeling empty and inferior. I read articles about how to succeed and tried to apply them, but I only grew more frustrated because I wasn't making any progress. Job after job, my career opportunities remained lateral. I thought I was stagnant—and to a certain degree, I was. I was stagnant in my perspective. I was attempting to attain success through the lens of quantity and upward mobility. I had not taken the time to recognize my worth or the value of my craft and what I had to offer. But with time (oh, thank goodness for time!), I realized that I wasn't stagnant in achieving success, my mind simply needed to reassess what success was. I had plenty of opportunities for accomplishments, but I was trying to cultivate constant victory for something that would continue to change. I wanted to show people that I was successful, but I didn't identify the value that I had to offer that was worth sharing. I was powerless only because I didn't understand the power of me.

Power at Bottom of the Chain

The bottom of the food chain doesn't equate to

zero optimism, laziness, or a non-dreamer. You can be content or frustrated– but plants have demonstrated that regardless of how we feel, we have the potential to make an impact. People who are at the bottom of the food chain work very hard, but their work does not necessarily reap the benefits of upward mobility. But there is so much development that can happen, as with any plant– the development begins before we can see change, but to the budding plant the development has been taking place for some time.

When it comes to having power at the bottom of the food chain it starts with understanding that your self-worth can make you worth it. It will take deliberate actions by you for things to transform from a powerless position to be one of the most influential, without a change in status.

Plants at the bottom of the food chain are the foundational basis. These plants at the bottom also complete the process of photosynthesis—but there is more. Those plants at the bottom are classified and given a name, and of all the names to have, *Power Producer* is the title bestowed to those located at the bottom.

There is nothing weak about that name. And

that is just the beginning. Power Producers can sustain their own life, other lives, and they provide nutrients to all life forms, but the key is that they must first create their own energy–photosynthesis. Even though they are at the bottom placed in the path of consumption, Power Producers create and transfer power to improve the overall environment—their role contributes to the overall success.

There would be no way to keep the flow of the pyramid if Power Producers didn't sustain. How is this reflective of ourselves? There may be much frustration at the bottom of the chain with a desire to move upward or you may be content with where you are. However, bitterness, discouragement, and complacency cannot cultivate the potential that Power Producers create. Power Producers, make the most of their environment and create something that is worth sharing. Each organism moving upwards from the bottom level benefits from the properties of organisms at the bottom of the food chain.

Some creatures eat Power Producers directly, such as omnivores and herbivores, while others eat them indirectly, such as carnivores. Even though Power Producers' placement in the hierarchy displays that they are underneath all other levels, their placement also demon-strates that they are the influential starting point for success. And their ability to create their own power, and share it is a superpower that not many people talk about.

This is a power with many benefits so I want to share with you three elements that I have classified as fundamentals that will guide you to recognize that you are worthy in the workplace. If you believe yourself to be at the bottom of the food chain as a Power Producer–you are no less. You are enough. And these fundamentals will help you to see your potential and value that as in-valuable and redefine success so that you will no longer need to correlate your position, status, appearance, inner circle on how worthy you are. The three elements are:

- Sustainment
- Growth
- Contribution

These are elements that are needed for the plant kingdom to succeed and that are also needed for *you* to succeed in understanding your worth.

The Fundamentals

Sustainment is focus, maintenance, and exis-tence. When it comes to the plant kingdom, sustainment is about the importance of the existing, taking up space, and maintaining. For us, as humans, sustainment is consistently recognizing and identifying your value, your worth, your craft(s) and what you have to offer. With sustainment you understand the overall goal and make the connection of how your role can provide impact.

Here is an example to provide some clarity, a five-star hotel can only be so hospitable if housekeeping and janitorial staff refuse to believe that their efforts contribute to the success by providing a clean and healthy environment that can eliminate germs that can cause illnesses. Every person involved at every level is responsible for the prominence of that hotel, just like every organism in one food chain is responsible for the glory of the lion. But the key is understanding how each level affects the overall goal. And to make that impact, you have to first sustain and sometimes this takes place in your workplace, sometimes it's your home, and some-times it's in your community.

Whatever your role in a company or community, it is essential that you discover *and* acknowledge what you have to offer. Focus on yourself and be clear as to how, and what you bring to the table that adds to the overall success, not just for you but for others as well; otherwise, it will be hard to grow and share your craft with others.

The next element is growth. Growth for plants begins internally before you or I can see the changes that are already happening. Plants, like you and me, are living things. For growth, plants take in energy from the sun and use it to make food (photosynthesis). Using nutrients from the soil, they grow into young plants and become adults. They also have the potential to create new plants by growing seeds. Each plant is unique and different from all the others. But all plants share the need of light, air, moisture, temperature, and nutrients.

Growth for plants encompasses so much, including the need for healthy roots, water, soil, sun, and all other nutrients required to be effective. It is the same for you, your growth is based on your efforts: where you place your focus (energy), your surroundings, what you invest in, how you educate yourself. The actions you take to increase your learning. Development or growth is about ways of improvement. The focus with growth is on the work that can be done in you that will build on what you have sustained to make you more effective at what you do. Ultimately, growth is about developing yourself.

And finally, contribution. This is an external action. For plants, this is sharing the oxygen created and sharing the nutrients that are created to provide life for others. After a plant completes photosynthesis, it doesn't benefit others unless it is shared with others. As human beings, the contribution is taking your skills and ability that you have identified and effectively grown and sharing it with others where they are able to grow from what you shared. While this one is the least complex to explain, it requires the most effort as it requires the other two elements to be in process and consistently in progress for the contribution to be effective.

For a more concrete understanding of how all three elements work, let's look at a stay-at-home parent as an example. This is someone who in my opinion works tirelessly to get the job done. I have had the privilege of being a stay home parent full-time, and it exhausted me. Primarily because I was never done. My response when communicating with a 9–to–fiver was usually, "Oh, you get off at 5 pm? That's nice. I get off….never." And honestly, I didn't think that what I did was important. No one was telling me, "Thank you."

I wasn't making any money from it. And I constantly saw my peers with paid jobs receiving promotions, buying nice things, and having babysitters. But through sustainment, growth, and contribution, I developed an understanding of my worth and the value and influence my role had.

The sustainment was to recognize that *nurturing* is one of the many significant responsibilities of a stay-at-home parent, where the goal is to raise a mature adult. Growth was me discovering how to improve how I nurture—be it through educating myself, self-care, support groups, or other means. And finally, contribution—sharing my developed skills, approach, and ability by nurturing my children and potentially sharing what I learned with others. These actions ultimately led to positive changes in my children and the ripple effects are still coming. Their lives were affected by being nurtured as were the other individuals who were able to partake in the knowledge and experiences shared.

As I mentioned earlier, and as we will speak more on in Chapter Five–every organism has a different journey and a different way to contribute. Even though my sustainment, growth, and my interpretation of my contribution is one way, the power in which you decide to sustain, grow, and contribute is up to you. The core focus is about you understanding that you have merit, and you are worthy enough to offer it. You don't need to wait for a degree, certification, or promotion to make something happen (unless it's illegal to do so).

The plant kingdom needs three things to thrive: sustainment, growth, and contribution. While organisms such as grass, trees, moss, plankton, and more might look like passive organisms that just sit and wait, plants have a lot more power than that. And thus, using these same elements as a basis will help you realize your worth. Your position now has no bearing on what you have to offer. You may have sacrificed time, money, family, and more to reach a goal that never came to be, but success is not determined by the fulfillment of that goal. As we cover sustainment, growth, and contribution in more detail over the next few chapters, you will have the opportunity to explore how these actions can aid you and supply the nutrients needed to make an impact, starting at the bottom of the food chain. We will start with a closer look at the many definitions of the bottom of the food chain and what that can mean for you. But first I want to encourage you to reflect on what we have talked about so far.

Reflection

Ask yourself the following questions and write your answers:

1. What opportunities are available for me to make an impact?

2. What can I change in my environment if I made an impact?

SEA ECOSYSTEM

CHAPTER THREE
ECOSYSTEMS OF IMPACT

What is more powerful: A whale or a polar bear?

Neither and both.

They are both powerful in their own right, but what makes the biggest difference are their ecosystems. If given the opportunity to live in each other's ecosystem on an extended basis, the outcome will be based on each location.

The same is applicable in the workplace and your placement in the food chain. You may be at the top of your game in one setting, but in that same breath, add a person or two and subtract a person or two, and you could very well shift to the bottom. The environment is one of the primary determinants of this predicament, and it is always changing, but if you feel that you are worthy, no external change will affect what you can offer.

Before I continue, I want to address the importance of the bottom of the food chain. When I initially brought up the idea of the bottom of the food chain and stated that certain positions would fall into the bottom, some of you reading this may have thought that it was rude and presumptions of me to classify some positions at the bottom of the food chain and others as at the top. And while I do understand that perspective, I want to bring it to light and hopefully change the perspective that is already in place.

The US Bureau of Labor Statistics demonstrates society's value of certain jobs over others, with positions such as physicians, lawyers, pilots, marketing managers, and developers being listed as some of the highest-paid occupations. At the other end of the spectrum, jobs such as food preparation, janitorial, and administrative staff are listed as the lowest-paid occupations. Also, when you conduct an online search using terms such as "top 100 jobs" or "top 50 jobs," results will display like those previously listed. These lists confirm the idea that certain jobs come with prestige, and in a way authority to be declared successful.

It's natural for us to have a desire to be in a position that is of high approval and acceptance—one of our long-term instincts for survival is social acceptance. However, it's important to be aware of this contingency and that many people base their self-worth on this fact.

According to a 2019 peer reviewed article, it was determined that social norms and influences were one of the primary influences of a career decision, meaning that jobs with more influential power and salary typically tend to be the deciding factors in influence and norms. Being at the bottom of the food chain is about challenging that status quo and providing an open perspective that requires us to not only see the importance of ourselves and our self-worth, but also to acknowledge the opposing thoughts.

To focus on being at the bottom of the food chain is not typical and generally not desired. But, there is much to be said about what comes from the bottom, or the basis. In this chapter, we will take a closer look at the examples as to what defines the bottom of the food chain, as we examine them through the lens of ecosystems.

An ecosystem is an environment where a particular energy pyramid exists. Each organism within that system interacts with one another, whether directly or indirectly. Each ecosystem has its way of completing that task at hand (a transference of energy), and each ecosystem knows what works and what does not work. Ecosystem is a term that has become relatively popular in the last ten years as companies used the phrase to describe a value chain where all interactions have the same goal or value. For both business and nature, sometimes the organisms or people overlap with other ecosystems.

In Chapter Two, I provided an example of a food chain/energy pyramid, starting with the grass and ending with a hawk. Those organisms are in a particular ecosystem, starting with the grass; they all affect each other. However, it's important to note that contributing at a certain level to one food chain does not eliminate contribution in another. For instance, hawks don't just eat snakes. Snakes eat more than mice. Mice eat other organisms besides grasshoppers. Grasshoppers eat more than one type of grass. And the grass grows in more than one location. Depending on the environment, each of those organisms can contribute to potentially different levels in different ecosystems.

To apply this, we can look at a common company organizational structure the same way. Starting from the bottom and working up: janitorial staff, administrative support staff, junior staff, senior staff, VPs, and CEO/COO. You can take any of these positions and place them in a different environment (ecosystem) and the new environment will potentially shift the level of authority or power. A CEO at a Fortune 500 company may be at the top of their food chain compared to the CEO of a new start-up with little to no investors. A janitor at a popular brand may rank higher than a janitor at an elementary school. Even though the general order of authority determines positions in the food chain, there are times when we can be at the top of the food chain in the environment, but one alteration can affect the change in process, communication, feedback, and power.

To further examine this, we can also take a university, college, and trade school for example. In an ecosystem consisting of all three institutions, a person who attends university is generally seen as being at the top of the food chain compared to community college or trade school graduates. In that same token, Ivy League Universities are at the top of the food chain compared to other schools throughout the country and world.

A lion and a whale can be at the top of their games. They can be at the top of their food chains in individual systems, but, when they are placed together, who will end up at the top? That would depend on the environment. An oak tree and krill are at the bottom in the same environment as a lion and a whale. But in an ecosystem where both the tree and the krill are together, who will be at the top of the game? Again, it would depend on the environment, the familiarity, the acquaintance, which one is better at adapting, which one can make the most out of the current situation.

It is the same with us. You could very well be at the top of the food chain in one environment and at the bottom of the food chain in another. And that is the power of ecosystems. However, you may feel that you are never at the top of the food chain or at the bottom, and you may not be. But it is still important to note that being at the top doesn't guarantee you will always be there. Nor does being a Power Producer guarantee you will always be one.

However, if you are a Power Producer, there is much to offer. You have value. You are invaluable. High visibility roles are not required to be important. Being at the bottom of the food chain doesn't mean you aren't good at what you do. There are thousands of undiscovered and talented musicians, artists, untrained engineers, and un-scouted superstar athletes. They are not at the top for many reasons, but thank goodness being at the top is not the determining factor of being successful or being worth something.

I write this book, this chapter, in a time of low visibility. I am an inspirational speaker and career coach. I know that what I share with others inspires and enlightens, but I am not booking speaking gigs left and right. My clients are not high-ticket clients. I do not have a large following on my social media platforms. Yet, I still have something to offer. Every day that I work with clients and share my message, I do so knowing that I have value. I have and can make a positive impact from a low visibility role because I am a Power Producer, and my impact flows throughout the food chain, as does yours. So here is another opportunity to reflect on how you can create impact, no matter your ecosystem. Ask yourself these questions and write your answers.

Reflection

1. Whether I am at the top of the game or a Power Producer, what do I do to create impact?

2. How do I define my impact?

CHAPTER FOUR
SUSTAINABILITY

If you have ever been on an airplane, you might have heard that, in case of an emergency, you need to first secure your own mask before helping others. That is because, if you wish to help others, there is a necessity first and foremost to tend to your needs and ensure you keep yourself alive. Bottom line: you cannot help others if you are physically unavailable. And the same is true for the bottom of the food chain: to produce and create impact, an organism must first be well, otherwise the ability to share energy is highly limited.

Sustainment is labeled as the first phase of becoming an influential Power Producer for that very reason, to sustain your energy chain, you must first sustain yourself. Plants are also Power Producers and supply around 90 percent of the world's food. Nearly all food sources and energy come from the bottom. Once you recognize that as a Power Producer in your work-place you also contain such influence, you recognize that you have something worthwhile to share, no matter what your position is. And once you care for yourself, growing and contributing will eventually become natural steps for you.

Sustainment and Self-Worth

Sustainment has three primary parts: seeing your self-worth, knowing yourself, and addressing your values.

Self-worth is a conscious focus and determination—valuing yourself and identifying, understanding, and maintaining your impact power. Many people often use self-worth and self-esteem interchangeably, but there are differences to note. John Niland, the author of *The Self-Worth Safari*, describes the difference as this: "Self-esteem may require us to live up to certain values, but self-worth does not. Self-worth can be accessed even on those days when we are not doing what we 'should'."[1] Essentially, self-worth is how we view ourselves, a constant and unconditional love and friendship with ourselves—as Niland described.

Whether we accomplish something or not, we are worthy, and even better is that we are at the same level of worth. You reach your goal, that's fine, you are

---

[1] John Niland, The Self-Worth Safari: Valuing Your Life and Your Work (VCO Academy, 2019), 88.

worthy and deserving. You don't reach your goal, that's fine, you are worthy and deserving. That sounds a lot like Power Producers to me, organisms who can sustain their worth regardless.

Unlike self-esteem, self-worth doesn't shift based on how you view yourself. Having high self-worth is being fully aware of who you are and how amazing you are, no matter the change to your external situation. Low self-worth also exists, and it is believing that you are unworthy or undeserving no matter what you do. The goal is to sustain a high sense of worth.

When you sustain, you are aware that you deserve to take up space, you deserve to rest, or work, because regardless of what comes of your goals, you are worthy. To sustain is to remain strong and perhaps to remain where you are. This doesn't mean that sustaining is against improvement, quite the opposite; sustaining is about acknowledging that whether you succeed or fail, you are worthy. You walk into a room as the person with the least accomplishments or the most rejections, and yet you realize that you have just as much value to bring as everyone else in that room. Knowing your worth is sustaining.

Sustainment and Knowing Yourself

Let's have another quick review on the science lessons that we had in Chapters Two and Three. The organisms located at the bottom are Power Producers and can create power and disperse it. They can construct an atmosphere better not only for themselves, but also for others. Therefore, whether we are considering the animal kingdom or our lives as humans, the bottom of the food chain contains massive strength. Because of the power at the bottom that directly and indirectly maintains life as great as it does, the bottom level must be sustained.

According to Merriam-Webster, sustainability means "using a resource so that the resource is not depleted or permanently damaged."[2] Think about how Power Producers are able to not only provide an essentialness to the food chain but even more so how these organisms need to properly balance that. This requires each entity in the plant kingdom to be aware of themselves to effectively grow and thrive. Think of the many plants throughout the world, who supply us with energy in different ways. Starting out as a seed, buried in the soil, seeds still can find the correct path to grow. Plants

2   Merriam-Webster.com Dictionary, s.v. "sustainable," accessed April 6, 2022, https://www.merriam-webster.com/dictionary/sustainable.

have a self-assembling process where each seed can grow in a particular direction. This innate ability allows plants to sense their environment and develop roots in a downward direction and sprout upward toward the sunlight. The reason that stems grow upward is because the plant knows it needs sunlight for photosynthesis. This type of awareness also applies to root growth; roots know they need to dig deeper to absorb nutrients, so they dig downward.

For you, knowing yourself is a commitment to focus on you. An introspection of your thoughts, fears, truths, and so much more can reveal who you truly are and what you are truly capable of. A major part of that is addressing your needs.

Weeds

When you sustain, you take the time to focus on your essentials. This can give you the opportunity to find the weeds in your life. It's easy to get wrapped up in the hustle and bustle of life that you fail to be intentional about your desires. You may forget to address those things that will add value to your energy due to the distractions that can deplete your energy and prevent you from sustaining.

A weed, in a scientific definition, is a plant that is not where it should be. So, if you are growing a bush of dandelions and roses start to grow, no matter how beautiful a rose may be, in this environment, it is a weed. When roses and dandelions grow in the same soil, unplanned, they are fighting for space and nutrients. They are fighting for power and the opportunity to grow— and the goal is to live and thrive. Through reflection, the same can be stated for your career and the weeds that may try to invade your worth and impact.

Whenever you focus on your goals as a Power Producer, weeds can sneak in and take away your nutrients, thus preventing you from being an effective Power Producer. Let's say that you are in a career transition from a long-time career in teaching to one of instructional design. If you want to increase your understanding and ultimately land a job where you can utilize that knowledge, your focus must be on the steps required to cultivate a new and fulfilling career. In this case, weeds could be the thoughts surrounding your loss of professional identity: no longer an educator, and so you may have taken on work in the interim, or you no longer have a desire for the work that you do. The weeds slowly creep in and may attempt to deplete your energy with self-inflicted criticism, or the influences of external noise that tells you are no longer worthy, and you can no longer make a difference.

Weeds are ideas or actions that prevent you from recognizing what you are capable of in your career. Particularly with the objective of finding career fulfillment. Weeds appear when you don't reach your goal. Your self-doubt and shame start to tell you that your lack of reaching your goal is reflective of who you are and your value.

Addressing Your Values: Roots & Soil

Weeds are not the only challenge to your sustainment. Ensuring proper rooting and the correct soil are essential elements, and the benefits are similar to our values. Roots are impactful to the growth of any plant because before the budding begins, the roots are established. Knowing that sustainment, growth, and contribution are possible because of your foundation, rooting makes the health of your roots even more essential. Roots grow over time and the soil is a big part of that, as together they can influence growth from the inception.

Your values (or roots and soil) provide guidance, inspiration, and stability, creating and instilling a foundation from which your actions and decisions are shaped. Your values, like the roots of a plant help keep you grounded and give you strength in difficult times.

As a Power Producer, I can't emphasize enough how powerful you are. Your values serve as roots and soil to that power. Those values nourish you and provide healthy nutrients to that soil. It may be hard to connect how your values can significantly affect your self-worth when it comes to your career but doing so can provide some clarity and help you to find new and healthy ways to increase your self-worth, regardless of where you are in your career. Knowing your values can clarify and pinpoint what works for you in your career or personal life. If you value something that is not present or you dismiss what you value, it can leave you unfulfilled.

To sustain is to get down to the root of the matter (pun intended) and get to know you. If I ask you, "What are your reasons to work in the field that you are in now?" You would most likely have a different answer than someone else who also works in the same field. Your answer can reveal so much about who you are: it explains what you care about, what you know to be true, your values.

Your values plant you where you are and keep you planted if you remain true to them. Your values may change over time, but the key is to know what they are. Continue to sustain through recognition of your values and give them space to be rooted.

A few years ago, I secured my dream job (or so I thought). After a year of working there, I did not have the satisfaction that I had dreamt of. I felt very much alone and felt no connection with my coworkers. I felt like what I did was insignificant. Perhaps it was the lack of, "Thank you," from the people I was helping. Or maybe it was the fact that nothing that I said held any weight. There was someone with more authority, who could say the exact same thing, and then it would become a priority. I felt unappreciated. I gave my heart and soul to my job to change lives, but it didn't feel like it mattered to anyone. I was miserable and I knew that I needed to get to the root of the problem. So, first thing, I did some self-exploration to determine what the issue was. Easy: I dreaded work. Next, I tried to figure out why I dreaded work. I was making well above the national average salary but, there was still no fulfillment. I had wonderful coworkers, but I felt like no one cared if I left or stayed. I knew my job well enough to complete my assignments, but I was bored. When I closely examined my behavior, I noticed it all tied back into my values or the lack thereof. My fulfillment came through meeting my value of connection. I didn't have that at work. When I started that job, the salary was the primary motivator why I wanted that position. This is not to say that prioritizing money is wrong, but it was not something I valued. Placing money before everything else did not fulfill me, because it is not a rooted desire for me.

What I didn't know at the time was that I was a statistic. Research has shown that job satisfaction rarely comes from money alone; it comes from the fulfillment of a career that brings us joy and pride. Remaining true to your values is one of the most secure ways to be fulfilled.

I didn't immediately see the link between my values and my career contentment, but once I explored it, it was clear. It wasn't a vertical career progression that I needed. I simply needed to move forward in my job—I needed career adjustments with connections. I needed my values met. I needed to be sustained.

If you have had a similar experience, I recommend identifying your values so that you can sustain them, and they can sustain you. If you are not sure what your values are, these questions can start the process to help you identify them:

1. Something I appreciate about my workplace is:

2. Something that is important to have in my work-place is:

3. These are the things that make me proud to work where I work:

This is just a start, but after further exploring and determining your values, you can determine how your career/workplace can meet those needs within reason. Taking the time to clarify your values and identify and appreciate what you have to offer increases your self-worth because *you* have assigned significance to you. You know how you bring value because you have identified what you value.

As a Power Producer, you can transfer the energy of knowing your worth through your craft. Your energy rooted in your skills, can make a world of a difference, not just for you but for others within the same environment as you.

Our Sustainment Goes Back to Nature

Imagine a world with no Power Producers: plants, trees, grass, algae, phytoplankton, all within the plant kingdom, gone. Only destruction would ensue if there was only consumption and no replenishment. Such a world of depletion would not take long for total extinction to occur.

This is true for animals as well as humans: when there is sustainment, something can create its own energy and share it as necessary to keep things moving. This is an important part of the foundational basis. We have looked at the pyramid and the strategic placement of the Power Producers, but even with that placement, if Power Producers aren't able to keep themselves alive, their placement is not effective. As a Power Producer, it is important for you to know yourself, take care of yourself, and identify what you have to offer.

There is something to be said for work and effort that is put in, regardless of what position or title it leads to. To sustain is to create the influence and power that is needed to maintain life.

Look at this upside-down energy pyramid below. The way that it is positioned, if the energy continues to flow upward, it will fall. There is not enough power to keep it standing. Many may want to reach the top, but there is significance at all levels.

Think of anything that has a bottom. What would happen if you were to take away the bottom? Shoes without soles aren't any good for protection. A pitcher without a bottom can't hold water. I have tried to sit in a chair with a missing leg and guess what? That didn't work out. Think of what would happen if there were no teachers, janitors, nurses, receptionists, or assistants. And this is only a few of the positions considered to be on the bottom. Without someone in those roles, there would be an inability to complete additional work within the company or organization, thus unable to

THE FOOD CHAIN

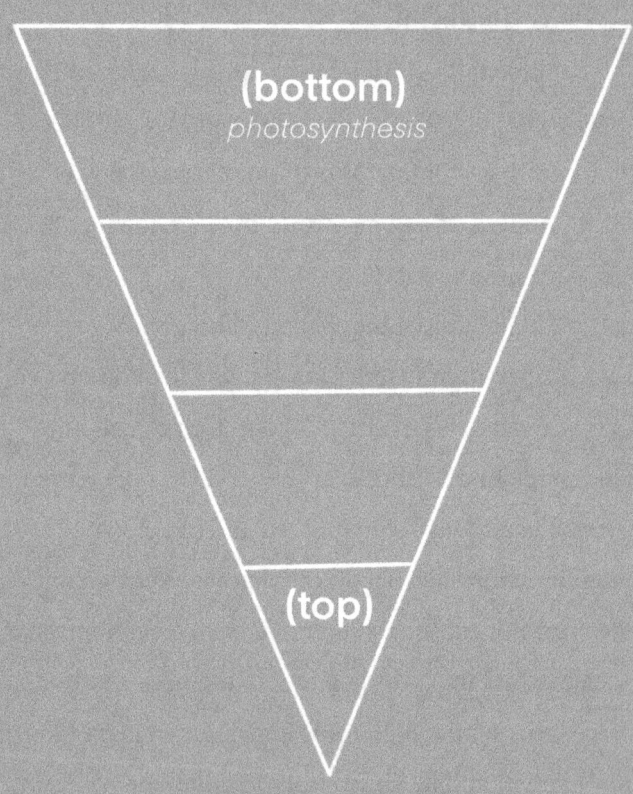

(bottom)
photosynthesis

(top)

achieve the overall goal. The bottom is important. No, scratch that. The bottom is essential! You are essential!

When you say the bottom of the food chain, it can sound so harsh because we have seen and heard the bottom as being less than. You may have experiences where you were treated or referred to as less than for whatever reason. But the bottom of the food chain is the home of the Power Producers. The bottom of the food chain supplies life from the beginning and throughout. And just like the bottom food chain level can succeed once it has established itself, if you sustain through caring for yourself and recognizing and identifying what makes you worthy, you will be one step closer to victory.

If you aren't quite sure what it is that you have to offer, it's okay. You can speak with a trusted friend or colleague to get started, and you can have them assist you with these reflection questions at the end of this chapter.

In my past, I failed to see the significance of being at the bottom and it took me years to understand that even with rejection from promotions and social circles I still had something to offer. You, too, have something to offer. I hear from so many people that you learn from mistakes, but they don't have to be *your* mistakes, so let me save you time. Consider this a lesson learned, don't fail to see the potential in who you are. Sustain.

Reflection

Here are some questions that can help you start the process to recognize the value that you can bring and identify how important you are. Take some time to ask yourself these questions and write down your answers.

1. Three characteristics that I like about myself. (These are internal characteristics—e.g., strong-willed, ambitious, direct, curious, and loving.)

2. Answer the following questions about your characteristics:

    a. Why is that attribute important to me?

    b. How does this attribute influence my life?

3. Choose a few trusted people and ask for their feedback:

    a. What words do others use to describe me?

    b. What do others think are my strengths?

CHAPTER FIVE
GROWING PAINS

Science riddle: What takes an average of thirty years for trees, but phytoplankton can double in a day? Growth.

Okay, so that may not be the best riddle, but the point remains: across the world and throughout many life forms, growth occurs in different types and times. Humans and most animals are born with all their body parts and as they grow and mature, their body does as well. However, research has shown that for plants, the process is slightly different.

As plants go through the process and several phases of growth, they consistently develop over time. Through their development, new tissues and structures are created, molding a vastly different result than when it first started.

Taking another note from the plant kingdom, our growth is not about having everything upfront, it is about maturing some things, adding others, and perhaps even shedding or eliminating some aspects that do not help us to maintain a healthy version of ourselves.

Growth, the second phase of becoming a Power Producer, is a constant. By *growing,* I am referring to strengthening and evolving what has been identified in sustainment. This can come in many forms. Growth comes from unlearning things, asking for help, setting boundaries, and experimenting with ways to improve. Through it all, it is about making a progression to move forward, while developing respect and trust for yourself.

Growth is not the aim for perfection. It's not about outgrowing your competition or becoming the best of the best. Growth, within self-worth, is knowing that you are enough, and being confident in the knowledge that being worthy doesn't mean that there isn't something you can do to be stronger.

In general, there are five elements required for a Power Producer to grow: light, air, moisture, temperature, and it aids in creation of nutrients, which is the fifth element. A combination of these elements will alter, challenge, expedite, or perhaps even prevent growth. As a human Power Producer, it is up to you how much of each element is needed for you to apply. Let's look at some of the many elements involved in growth and explore them in greater detail.

Take a look at plants and where each one is planted. When organisms are planted and nurtured properly, they grow. If the needs of organisms are ignored, it could negatively affect the plant's overall growth.

Think of a water-based organism such as phytoplankton planted in-ground soil, the likelihood of that working is slim. And even if it did work, you would have to wonder if the right impact is being made. Phytoplankton needs certain things to grow, mature, and build momentum. Once again, organisms provide us with insight for things to remember as Power Producers.

But let's focus on each element necessary for plants to grow and share ways that similar attributes could affect our lives. This may get a bit technical, but I hope you're ready.

The Element of Light

Light, sunlight, or artificial light are one of the most essential elements for the plant kingdom, because it is through light that the process of photosynthesis is created. Photosynthesis is the process where energy is converted from light to energy, and this energy will be needed for the entire pyramid. Without light, plants would not be able to produce energy. Light is a realizable opportunity for growth. If you see an opportunity for growth, this is your light, the ability to take a given situation with a positive mindset as a driving force to grow and eventually contribute.

The unique thing about light and growth is that the light received doesn't have to be direct, and it doesn't have to be bright. There is a certain level that must be present, and the amount is dependent on the Power Producer. If you are the Power Producer faced with potential opportunities for growth, you must determine what will help you to grow.

The Element of Air

Plants need carbon dioxide and in return, they give us oxygen, creating a cyclic effect of life. To breathe in and out is all about balance. Too much oxygen for a plant is not a good thing, neither is too little. The goal is not to suffocate the plant, the goal is to provide proper room, space, and location for the plant to breathe. Think of air as your boundaries, this is your ability to balance. This is an opportunity to determine how much to give, both now and later to establish and maintain growth.

When you don't protect your boundaries, you run the risk of not growing. Whether it's growing too fast or not fast enough. The thing about growth is that even though it is the second phase, it is a continuous simultaneous connector. As a plant sustains it also grows, and as it grows it also contributes. Therefore boundaries, or air, is an important element. As you grow, you may need to catch your breath (catch some air). But at the same time, extended breaks can also be detrimental to growth. The opportunity to establish growth in the past, present, and future comes from setting healthy boundaries.

The Element of Moisture

Dew, droplets, mist, rain, ocean, any body of water that provides life for the plant kingdom is moisture. Water can be symbolic of knowledge, strength, direction but ultimately moisture is something that prevents plants from becoming thirsty, dry, or weak. As with the other elements, moisture must strike a balance to be effective. Too little or too much of anything can be detrimental.

It's great to have knowledge, but what happens if you only gain knowledge or strength (lots of it), but you don't apply it? Or if you don't step away and evaluate what you've learned? With all the knowledge you have, you still may feel that you are no longer worthy of your job. Knowledge is meant to strengthen you and to help you create strategies to sustain and not to change you because you feel unworthy. Knowledge comes with balance.

We gain knowledge through the books we read, through the connections we cultivate with others, through life experiences. You need to find what works best for you. This can also include an unlearning—realizing that perhaps what you were once exposed to was not the best for you, such as that self-esteem mindset that keeps you striving for a standard that is unattainable for you, and it causes you to feel like you are never enough. It's important for you to find a new approach, if necessary.

The Element of Temperature

Temperature for plants determines if something is too cold or too hot to grow. There are ideal climate temperatures for maximum potential growth. And the same is for us. There are ideal climate temperatures that can help us to grow. When you feel challenged, but not violated or overused, there is still much work that can be done. However, when those challenges overwhelmingly build and you don't allow yourself the opportunity to step away from the pressure, it causes harm not only to you but to your entire ecosystem. So, if the pressure becomes too much, it's okay to step away. Too much heat can burn a plant, and not enough heat can whither it. Gage how much pressure works for you when it comes to finding ways to grow your value.

The Element of Nutrients

The final element is nutrients. Nutrients bring a unique addition, because not only are nutrients created from exposure to the other elements, but nutrients are also created based on space, location, time, and soil. This can be representative of the mindset, self-talk, relationships, and environment that leads to nutrients such as educating yourself, finding a support system, gaining feedback, unlearning and experiential learning, and more. This is about finding something that can edify what you do. When it comes to your nutrients there are multiple things that you need to grow, but how you go about it depends on your goal, and what you have access to. What can create a growth opportunity for you?

As a Power Producer, you are a part of a designated ecosystem, a company, or affiliation. Chances are you will find yourself in a role that may not offer you promotion opportunities or offer the possibility for more rewards. The opportunity for *growth* is still there, but you'll never know unless you take the time to identify how you can make that happen. So often we get into a rush of getting out of a job we don't like. I have been there. I couldn't sleep at night because I didn't want to wake up and repeat the workday. I hoped that no one had a question and I prayed that the internet would not work so that I didn't have to check my emails. I would literally go to work to hide and not be "bothered." The outlook was more exhausting than the job itself. Even if you are looking for employment opportunities elsewhere, finding ways to make the most of what you have in the interim is growth.

If you desire, you can still focus on how to upskill what you already have. If there is a healthy environment conducive to learning, take that time to learn how you can improve the delivery of what you have to offer. You see, self-worth is recognizing that you are amazing and wonderful and that you have something to offer just as you are. Your growth comes when you find modes to offer what you have.

So how about we take another look at the plant kingdom to see the application of the elements. There are perennial plants, with an extensive life typically lasting longer than two years. Biennial plants have a two-year growth cycle. Annuals grow in each season and die in each season. Each plant can grow and flourish by using the elements (light, air, moisture, temperature, and nutrients). However, there are cases when a shift in the elements can affect the life cycle. A popular perennial, such as a hibiscus, typically able to last through the year for multiple years. Hibiscus needs bright light with some direct sunlight daily. During the winter it can thrive in temperatures around 55 degrees Fahrenheit, but a shift in the temperature into the low 20s will place this plant at risk of death. No longer able to produce, no longer able to sustain, grow, or contribute. This is a reminder of the importance of the constant balance of elements for each Power Producer. The growth never stops, the elements that we need evolves.

Just because you have learned to appreciate what you have to offer (sustainment), doesn't mean that you will be satisfied or content with where you are in life.

Self-worth doesn't mean that you lack ambition or that challenges are no longer present. In fact, very few people are content with making progress *and then stopping*. What you can do instead is find a way to progress. Like Power Producers that require proper nutrients to sustain and grow, you will require this on your journey.

Different Growth for Different Folks

When it comes to growth, not every organism is the same. There is no one size fits all. Each one of us is different: we are in different locations and times in our life so how much we require of each element is different but utilizing each of the elements will be beneficial to our growth.

Within the plant kingdom, different producers provide different benefits throughout various ecosystems. Trees of sorts provide a large base of oxygen and improve the overall air quality, they can conserve water, and support wildlife. Moss assists with water absorption, soaking up water and then releasing it as necessary. Along with all the nutrients and all the different purposes, each organism on the bottom level requires different levels and types of care to grow. If you water a bamboo plant as you would a tulip, you may not have a plant—not a live one anyway. And what about those poinsettias that are extremely popular during the winter months, especially December? In most places, the winter is not the proper time to plant them in your yard—I learned that the hard way. All Power Producers need nutrients and it's important to consider how they obtain those nutrients and how much it varies from one organism to the next. The same is for us, what has worked for me, will not work for you. It's important to make that distinction, but what is also important to clarify is that as Power Producers you require nutrients. Look at a cactus, with over 2,000 types of this species, the approach that the cactus takes to collect nutrients is very different. With no leaves, it captures moisture and nutrients via its prickly stems instead of leaves. With no rain, yet fog, it captures enough moisture for the cactus to trap and later expend that energy.

You can be so focused on others, thinking that because you started your career at the same time as someone else that you should be where they are. You have admiration for the bloom that others are experiencing in their careers, but you don't realize how you are worthy, where you are. So, you can get caught up in trying to reach a standard that is not attainable because you are not the same. The blooms of an herb and flower are both useful, and worthy of taking up space, but they serve different purposes.

Some years ago, I kept greenery in my office, and in passing, people would compliment me on their upkeep. I would smile and say, "Thank you." Until one day, someone asked me how I could keep my flowers so beautiful all year round, at which point I responded with a smile, "They're fake." My coworker's mouth dropped. No one had asked me what I had done, or how I got there. No one knew that it took a ten-minute drive and $25 dollars (plus tax) to keep that plant alive. Oh, and an occasional wipe down with soap and water. The point is that looking to others to determine what success looks like isn't the most definitive or productive goal for growth. We can be inspired by others, but to use others as *the definition* can create aspirations that can only be desired and not achieved, thus setting you back into low self-esteem if you fail to reach or surpass it.

Don't go chasing…

Bringing your value to the workplace is not about checking off accomplishments. Bringing your value is about you, bringing what you have to offer and the development in your journey. Making strides from one step to the next. And take note that the movement doesn't require you to move upward to meet that goal, it only requires that you move forward. If actions are taking place, you are making progress.

Our societal standards have placed an emphasis on upward mobility for success. However, that is not always required, and sometimes as fate would have it, upward success is not always attained from hard work. Sometimes it's just the opposite, where success is attained or realized from not reaching the top.

As a kid, I greatly desired to be famous, to be a star. I wanted to be a famous actress. When I was sixteen, I competed in two nationwide competitions, one for acting and one for singing. For both, I won the competition at the local level. I was featured in local media outlets, it was announced at school, and people knew my name! But the feeling only lasted for a moment. After all of that investing of time and money, and practicing, I lost both competitions at the national level. I was crushed. There was no fame for me. My life returned to normal. I no longer believed I could be successful because I failed at attaining that version of success even with all the efforts I put forth. That scenario rolled over into adulthood. And constant chase for external factors to prove my success continued. There were many times when I worked to become successful. I wanted the promotion. I wanted the salary increase. I wanted the attention. I gave it everything I knew, but it wasn't enough to get me to the top and my self-esteem suffered because of it. I had tied my success to external factors that I couldn't reach, because every time I got closer, those factors changed. I kept chasing my dream, hoping that it would fill the void, but the void was the lack in me not seeing me.

There is so much work placed in each of our journeys, why should the result be the only praise point? Power Producers are not beneficial only after they have finished growing, they are beneficial from the start. I like okra, so I will use this as an example. Okra in full bloom is gracious on the palate (fried or smothered). But okra has a beginning. Even when it is a seed it is a beautiful beneficial Power Producer. The only difference is in *how* it is beneficial. As an okra lover, the seeds alone don't impress me, but I can name a handful of organisms that would be thrilled to have an okra seed! I am sure other animals throughout the food chain see the benefit at other stages. There are insects that benefit from the okra leaves, and deer that will enjoy the stems. Every step of growth creates an opportunity for benefit, the reward is not only at the final stage. Every phase of growth has a reward, even though it's not what we would typically expect.

When it comes to what you have to offer to make an impact, it's not determined by your upward movement in status or role in an organization. The results of your position, salary, or authority may be lateral. Lateral movement is not negative, because you are still making an impact.

To be fair, there are certain limitations when it comes to growth within some careers. The environment plays a huge part in accessing those elements. If several plants are fighting for light in a window, plants that are most hidden will adjust their growth to reach that light. This could result in extended branches or leaves, and while the plant with less light may be longer it may not necessarily be higher. For every job there will be natural limitations. The medical system has limitations on how much they can help patients. Schools have limitations on how much they can help students. Whether we agree with the limitations or not, they are there to meet certain end goals and require that we put in extra work to get the result we are aiming for.

So, what now?

Chances are this isn't the first self-help book you have read, and it won't be the last, but if you want this book or any other self-help book to work, you need to do one thing: act. For all perspectives and self-help books, mine included, nothing will ever change if you don't. You can read a book or two, get inspired, and then think about it and maybe even practice it to a certain extent, but then you reach a point where you are no longer interested. So, you stop.

Taking consistent action is the most assured way to see a difference. Even if you reach the "feel good" feeling, keep going, because when that feeling leaves if you have already started the journey and made some strides or started a momentum, you will be more likely to keep it going, even after the good feeling leaves. One of the largest types of trees, a Giant Sequoia, doesn't start off as a giant. It starts off as a seed and then over time, it grows to become something much different.

Growth is work, and growth is never done. Even though growth is preparation for another phase, it is still an action. It is an ever-active agent, so keep growing.

Reflection

As you take the initiative and time to grow, below are some questions to ask yourself and things to keep in mind that can help you to track your growth. Take some time to think and write down your answer to each of these questions.

1. The role and responsibilities where I am willing to invest time to grow are:

2. What areas in my current job do I see an opportunity for growth (e.g., education, support groups, resources)?

3. How am I investing in myself?

4. What actions am I taking to improve?

CHAPTER SIX
CONTRIBUTION

There are hundreds of millions, if not billions, of individual organisms at the bottom of the food chain. Each organism at the bottom of the chain, which is also known as Power Producers contributes to the overall ecosystem, in its own way and in its own time. As an individual who may be in an entry-level or junior level role in any particular ecosystem, or perhaps in a position that does not define you as the top, you are different from other Power Producers.

It's important to identify what makes you unique and highlight how you can contribute. Regardless of your position, everyone has something to offer. John Niland summed this up in his book, *The Self-Worth Safari*, "The more we drop our self-concerns the more room we have to be useful. We create space in which we can be curious, helpful, creative, and, as a result, successful."[1] When you decide that you are ready to get past the fear of others, whether it be rejections or opinions,

---

[1] John Niland, The Self-Worth Safari: Valuing Your Life and Your Work (VCO Academy, 2019), 248.

and offer your unique talents and abilities, it becomes valuable, but the key is in the offering. And the offering isn't to prove your worth, the offering is because you are enough.

In earlier chapters, we covered how to sustain and how to grow, but these two initial steps can only take you so far. What good are any of these things if we are unable to share with others? This step like the others requires action to keep things going.

Throughout this entire book, I have been using the analogy of the food chain as a deep reflection of what it may feel like being in a low visibility role and demonstrate the power of the bottom level. I am going to maintain that analogy as we move into the final phase, but now I would like to add in one element that we don't typically see from the plant kingdom, but as human beings, we have the capability. *You choose.*

Do you remember the pyramid that we discussed in earlier chapters? There is a gap there—two levels with blank spaces. This is for you. You sustain and create your energy, but to share what you have with others, you must decide how you will grow and contribute. At the back of this book is another pyramid (energy chain).

When the time is right, fill it in. When you find yourself in a workplace at the bottom, use the pyramid to discover how you can still make an impact if you choose to do so.

The Choice to Give

Throughout this book the plant kingdom has served as a potent reminder that there is sacrifice in being a Power Producer. Seaweed will produce and grow throughout its time; other organisms will come forth and take what they need to grow and continue to pass those nutrients and energy along the chain. But for us as human beings, we have an extra layer to add to that process. You have the ability to decide at any point if you will sustain your worth, grow it, or if you want to contribute what you have.

To commit and act on any of these three phases takes time and effort. This can be a scary decision, you may feel that you don't have anything to offer, so you may hold back the impact you can make. You aren't done growing so don't want to commit *just yet*. You recently learned a more effective way to accomplish a task so you aren't ready to share *just yet* because you can't answer all the questions. If the plant kingdom has shown us anything, it is that there is no time like the present. Seeds or baby-like forms of the plants are available from consumption from day one!

I remember many scarecrows growing up when my dad was in the process of growing whatever he could in the city on his homemade farm. Watermelon, sugar cane, corn, okra, collard greens, turnips, field peas, black-eyed peas, and more. The fact is, my father didn't wait until they matured to be attentive to them. At every phase of their growth, he had to remain watchful because there were always pests, animals, and even people that would try to take them away. Each phase of growth had an offering, an opportunity to contribute. Each stage had an impact potential.

And the same is for you and sharing what you have. You don't have to "be ready," because frankly, we won't ever be ready. And by the time you are ready, time may be up. So even now in the workplace, if you are just coming into the knowledge of your worth, you still have something worth giving. You have something that others will see as a benefit, and it requires nothing more than for you to recognize it, accept it, and then share it.

As the plant kingdom has shown us, the impact

isn't a one-time deal. Your impact is cumulative. Throughout your lifetime there are many moments that you can share something that can positively impact someone else. What you choose to contribute, or share will determine whether you make one impact or several. You are not limited to a one-time action. You can and most likely will, cross different ecosystems and keep making an impact. Our society looks for immediate results to determine what type of impact we make, but that can be very misleading. A reflection of a day in the life of organisms within the plant kingdom will showcase just how long it may take to see results!

But that's the catch: we look for the surface level, immediate results, but we don't always see the lasting reach. Like a wave, if we splash once, the wave will react but eventually it will die down. However, if we continuously splash, more water is affected, and its impacts will last longer.

Contribution Experience

Make your impacts intentional with purpose. Choose to make a positive difference. You choose what you want to offer, and you offer it with growth. Can you make a difference without intention? Yes, but what good is it. Without the intention, you don't know what good you are taking the action for. I can walk into a store and drop $100, unintentionally, and it will change someone's life. But where is the growth in that? But if I go into the store and I decide to pay for someone's groceries whether they know it or not, it is an intentional impact.

If I decide to smile at everyone, because I believe in the scientific studies behind sharing a smile, that is power. I am making a conscious decision, to share or contribute. You may have heard about the power in a smile. If you have not, research demonstrates that smiling not only increases the endorphins (happy chemicals) in you, but it also creates a relaxed and calming feeling. There is also a contagion factor as well. When you smile at others, it triggers something in the people who see you, mirror neurons. And those neurons are essentially a response to match an action that we see. And once we match that action, i.e., smiling, we can then feel the energy that comes with it, like happiness. You can also think about this when it comes to showing aggression in anger, or the infamous yawn. Those actions, have ripple effects. Your actions hold power.

Your energy focus can make an extraordinary

change in your workplace. So, it's important to determine the impact you want to make. If you decide to speak with your supervisor(s) about their actions you have to ask: Is this an opportunity to make a point and to be correct, or to benefit the future? Try to be intentional. Picking your battles, not just because you can win them, but because the impact is worth fighting for. My wonderful husband can attest to this, I have gotten upset and desired to speak my mind with no agenda because I just wanted to express how I felt. It didn't matter what the result was because I was right. And afterwards, there was no further action requested by me or taken because I just wanted to give them some "get right," as I call it. Basically, I was going to let someone know, so they realize they need to get it together, because I said so. However, with no purpose, the only impact made was probably trauma. A conversation with no purpose, just the ability to prove one person wrong, doesn't entirely create an impact. You can't ever guarantee that a positive impact will be taken or made if you are intentional, but if you gave a clear focus and purpose the chances of you making a change is possible.

Some years ago, I was taking my daughter to get

pizza as we were walking back to the car a gentleman tried to stop us and sell us something (I don't recall what it was). I was tired and paranoid, so I brushed him off and told him to leave us alone. I then proceeded to mean mug him as best I could. And then, just as I was about to get into my car, the man said, "I hope that your day gets better." There was silence. Those words stung me, but of course, I wasn't about to let him know that! Unless he reads this book and remembers that day, he will never know the impact he made.

Look at the plant kingdom, all the Power Producers are giving of their nutrients. The herbivores and omnivores nibble or entirely consume these producers and all the nutrients with them. They are taking it and utilizing it as they continue to keep the impact flowing in the food chain. This is what many have been waiting for; they are not only worthy, but they believe it enough to share it. Look at the following contributors and their contributions: the bus drivers, and all their patience in picking up children; the paralegal who, after using all their knowledge, passes it forward to the lawyers in court; the janitorial staff, who clean in order to keep everyone healthy and safe; within the group of board members with the least number of holdings sharing their insight; the stay-at-home parent gives their undivided attention to the devastation created due to the loss of the favorite teddy bear.

Your position doesn't limit you; it strategically places you to share. Contribution is sharing your skills, knowledge, and wisdom with others in a way that is useful. With each person, it may be a single or through increments, but either way with intention and consistently finding ways it will make a difference. Contribution is an action. It is an action for you that can benefit others. You can spend your time focused on reaching the top to be fulfilled. But in my experience reaching the top is like walking upward on a downward escalator, there is always something that can be done to go higher. But if you focus on making more impact on where you are, you will find yourself extending your reach.

However, nothing is so simple, right? But you also need to pay attention to your "impact roots," also known as your inner voice that is influenced by your experiences and expectations. Limiting beliefs can prevent you from challenging yourself to learn something new.

My Story of Contribution

One of my previous jobs was at a non-profit organization. This non-profit was operated by an Executive Board. The individuals on the board were the designated body to make decisions affecting the yearly operations and goals. As a volunteer for this non-profit organization, turned part-time employee, my influence was limited, but I somehow understood my power. I worked with clients who were homeless or living in poverty. I worked with people who were striving for better. When it came to my role at that organization, the board knew what my job description was, but not many could identify me in a line-up. But as one of the program coordinators, I saw the benefit that that program had for the agency. I recruited participants and mentors and created interactive training and engaged the clients. As uncomfortable as I was, I networked with other agencies within the community to get our clients started in a career and a new life. That dedication to not accept my title as a limitation, resulted in clients receiving employment opportunities. My clients received job offers from educational organizations, tech companies, and management companies.

For every person that successfully received

employment or assistance of any kind, there was a ripple effect in their lives, and it also benefited the organization I worked for. To some, my contribution may be seen as small, but I view it as a foundational factor that had a positive effect on people and programs. Just like every level of the food chain serves its purpose and importance, I served my purpose with that job. I was instrumental to that organization and the community, with or without recognition. My entire paycheck went to pay for childcare, and at times I wondered if what I was doing was right for me and our family. I am still not sure it was or wasn't, but that job gave me nutrients.

Every role can offer something. When you photosynthesize you are creating your energy, establishing your self-worth. Your value creates impact that exceeds any job title.

I am reminded of a story from one of my colleagues who spoke about the positive difference the mail delivery man made in her day. There was a connection developed. Through occasional doggy treats for my colleague's dog, this delivery man made a positive impact that went far beyond those conversations. Not only did it affect my colleague and her dog, but it also affected her family. And when she shared the story with me and others it impacted us as well. A delivery person made a huge impact, by taking the time to customize their deliveries with small touches of kindness. It was acknowledged how important not only the action but also the role or position, one that many may take for granted whether they work in the role or not.

And that is why self-worth is powerful. When you know that you are enough, and that your actions hold weight regardless of your title, you start to show that value to others. You contribute, which is a big part of keeping things balanced. If all Power Producers did was sustain and grow, the ecosystems still would not be able to operate effectively. An overwhelming amount of Power Producers would ultimately result in no power, and so contribution, or giving, is important.

Scientific Contribution

I would like to take you back to our science lesson that we covered at the beginning of this book and cover an additional element. When we take a closer look at our nature-based environment we can see how foundational elements, such as atoms, are required for expansion. Periodic table elements are basic foundational structures but when used and combined they create a bigger picture.

Our trusted Power Producers demonstrate this for us. You can think of many elements that are created at a foundational level: oxygen, sulfur, selenium, and more. These elements are unseen by our naked eye, and yet so powerful that our bodies would be deficient without an adequate amount.

The same can be said for your capabilities as a Power Producer: you may see yourself or your contribution as minimal, but how you bring value is significant to your workplace, because you have worth. You will not always see your impact, but it doesn't mean you don't create it. Your presence, your actions are needed.

Reflection

1. Some ways that I choose to bring value to my workplace or community are:

2. What do others say are the most helpful ways that I have helped them?

CHAPTER SEVEN
OBSTACLES & POTENTIAL

You may be skeptical about whether you can truly make a difference as a Power Producer. Perhaps you have been through disappointments in the past and no longer believe that things will work out as they should. You might think you don't amount to much, or you may fear that your family, colleagues, or coworkers won't care about what you have to offer.

I want to be honest and tell you that not everyone will recognize your power as a Power Producer, nor will they appreciate it. But it is not for others to embrace your ability to make an impact; it is for you. Self-worth is an internal value. It is something for each person to declare. If you fail to accomplish what you set out for, your worth does not diminish. It is also important to recognize that accomplishing those goals does not mean that you are worth more. You are always adequate. You arc always enough. Regardless of how you esteem yourself, you deserve to take up space. You will always have something to offer, no matter how much confidence you have. The doubt of others about you doesn't affect your potential.

A great white shark doesn't need to acknowledge green algae for green algae to be the powerful organism that starts the energy chain. Your potential is always present. Whether you work toward it, or away from it, it's there. Having self-worth in the workplace doesn't mean it comes without effort. Obstacles are a natural part of the process as they can slow things down or prevent things from moving forward altogether. There will be days, when you may feel that your self-worth and self-esteem are low, because of the rejection you face. When faced with a situation that is out of your control and that prevents you from following your plan, all you can do is tap into your potential.

Within the plant kingdom, Power Producers face difficulties in growing all the time. Detrimental weather, insects, infections, overconsumption or underconsumption from other organisms in the food chain, pollution, lack of elements mentioned in Chapter Five (light, air, temperature, moisture, and nutrients), are only some of the potential obstacles that plants must address to grow.

As you take on your role as a Power Producer, there will be many obstacles. In previous chapters, we covered how important your role is as a Power Producer. Power Producers work hard and put in the effort and though it may not be to the level of those we constantly see at the forefront, Power Producers make sacrifices. Being at the bottom of the food chain doesn't diminish what you have to offer. From CEO to customer representative and in between, you are one of the biggest assets to your workplace and community. Each employee has the power to transform the business into something better than it was yesterday. You are valuable. You are needed.

The Challenges

As essential as you are, I would be foolish not to address the obstacles of creating an impact while being at the bottom of the food chain. The first obstacles start with your mindset. Referring to yourself as being at the bottom of the food chain is not typically a phrase to convey power, because for the longest time many have viewed it as a position of little to no authority. But what are your reasons for believing that the top of the food chain is the only route to success? What is it about the brown bear that defines it as the most successful animal in its ecosystem? Your response might be that the bear has very few obstacles (in adulthood), and none other in that ecosystem will dare to bother it. But do you judge success based only on overcome obstacles? Not everyone who works hard or tries, makes it to the top. Not everyone who is persistent wins the gold medal. Not every great artist or musician who practices every day makes it into a prestigious school of arts. But it doesn't make them less successful, it doesn't mean they didn't work hard or that they have nothing to offer.

It can be easy to get into the mindset that because someone has more than you, you have nothing to offer. But that could not be further from the truth. People who teach us something are not always the people who have succeeded and excelled. Sometimes it's the people who tried and failed that can teach us. Sometimes it's the people who are still trying who can share what works. Sometimes it's the people who quit, who can encourage you to keep going. Offer what you can to who you can and allow them to benefit from your offerings. You won't always see the fruits of your labor, but if you make intentional decisions to move forward, you will become a key element that changes lives for the better.

Based on my experiences and from other individuals who I have seen excel at the bottom of the food chain in their careers, I want to share some of the obstacles you may face in addition to the many ways your potential as a Power Producer can help you to overcome those challenges. While the solution is not a one size fits all approach, there are some common obstacles that may come your way but with each of them comes the potential to address them.

Obstacle: Unused & Misused | Potential Is in Identifying

Unused and misused are elements that prevent you from reaching your ability to photosynthesize and see your worth. Being misused is having the properties to create something positive, but instead you ignore or create something based on what you feel your limitations are. As a human Power Producer, insecurities and low self-esteem can easily get you to that point. However, to make yourself useful in the workplace and to those around you, it's important that you identify those self-critical statements and address them. One of the ways to address this is to first reframe your mindset.

For anything to be used properly, you need to understand how it operates. I have had to put together a lot of items—furniture, toys, technological gadgets, the list goes on—but what usually gets me are the instructions. If I gloss over one step and use the wrong screw for the wrong part in the steps, the finished product is not pleasant.

A few years ago, I decided to take on the endeavor to put together a bookshelf. I was quite confident that I was able to complete this alone and I would have been successful had I done one thing: read the directions. In my haste, I skimmed through the directions, thus misusing several of the pieces. My final product turned out to be a shaky display of wood patched together, resembling a bookshelf that could only be used in a corner, leaning left, and without carpet. To keep it standing required a maneuver of sorts.

The moral of that story is, if you gloss over details in your life that you view as minimal because they don't give you the result you want, you may find that you are missing out on what you need. The tiniest of atoms, created something massive over time, every event, regardless of the magnitude, holds weight.

After completing several projects at work that reflected regionwide and even nationwide changes, my ideas were shared without me receiving recognition for them. I was overlooked for promotions, and at the time, I felt like I didn't have any value. I was unseen. But you see, if we are only looking for the visible results to prove that we are worthy or prove that we can make impact, we will miss the value that we bring. There will be many times when you will not receive praise for your efforts, and by no means do I recommend that you simply accept it. However, receiving recognition does not guarantee that you are making an impact.

To find your value, identify not the recognition of the action, but the usefulness of the action itself. This will help us to revive our self-worth amidst potential low self-esteem and to continue to positively affect the food chain and energy pyramid.

Obstacle: Unsure | Potential Is in the Possibility

Being unsure can prevent you from taking action but being unsure is normal. Uncertainty can make it difficult to act when you are unclear of the direction needed to take to get results. But the key is that any step you take will eventually lead you in the right direction if you are willing to evaluate your steps.

I had one client I will call, Billy. Billy decided that he wanted to take one route as he focused on communicating with his supervisor. Initially, he was unsure but that was the action he felt most comfortable trying. He had the conversation, and it was determined that his initial idea of staying with the company was not in his best interest. Things at work got worse, but he kept taking steps and eventually worked his way out of that situation. The first action he took wasn't wrong, but it wasn't the result he desired, so, he reevaluated and took another step. You see, even if you are unsure how to start creating an impact, you just need to start. As you take action, take notes, and evaluate what is going well and what can be improved, this will help you to determine your next steps.

Obstacle: Stunted growth | Potential Is a New Way to Grow

Plateauing in careers or improvement is an unfortunate yet common scenario. Many individuals may feel inadequate and held back because of company policy, restrictions, or rejections. There are two ways to address stunted growth: if the environments where the inability to grow are unhealthy, it may be time to reconsider if your work environment is detrimental to your mental, physical, emotional, and financial health. On the other side, if the inability to grow is happening in a healthy or otherwise neutral environment, the potential is in finding a creative way to grow where you are.

This type of growth may mean finding ways to change the quality of the setting you are in or change your environment altogether. Whatever that change is, remember that being a Power Producer is not limited to the workplace. Impacts can happen in any ecosystem, wherever you go and however often you decide to make impact it can happen. Try not to let a workplace situation limit your influence in other areas of your life.

When a plant is growing, if it is blocked from its initial route of sprouting, it will find alternative ways to sprout up, but that means it keeps growing. Sometimes you may not see the benefits until years later, but just keep growing.

Obstacle: You Cannot See a Difference in the Impact Made | Potential Comes with Time

You nor I can guarantee that anyone notices the impact we make. Whenever I am asked the question, "How did you get to this point in your life?" I can't narrow it down to just one moment because there are many that I remember, and others are more difficult to recall. For this book, so many factors contributed to me getting to the point of writing it: career positions where executives would disrespect my coworkers and me, times when people didn't think I knew what I was saying because I was "new"; the guy in the parking lot who wished me for better days; and the stories that people have shared with me.

For impact, you may look for immediate effect. We are a society that hinges on the "right now." But much like a Power Producer, we don't always see every change we make. Before we see the growth of most plants, the roots have established themselves underground. When you don't see the impact you make, if you are taking the actions to grow, change is happening, and impact is being made.

Obstacle: Rejection and Mistakes | Potential Is in Lessons Learned

Those times when you make suggestions in the workplace or in the community, and your idea is rejected; those times when you are consistently applying for jobs, but all you see is rejection. Rejection consists of the times when you have finally accepted that you are ready to be helpful and share your thoughts, but when you do so, no one seems to care. That is a painful experience, but it's important to continue sustaining, growing, and contributing and it is essential to find ways to learn from that rejection. Learning is not just what you can do differently but also looking at the situation as a whole and seeing what factors could potentially influence the result.

It may take years to see results at all, but that doesn't mean that results are not there. The product of self-worth is knowing that you still bring value, even with rejection and failure. You can get stuck in a black and white mentality where it is terrible if something goes wrong, and if something goes well, all is good. But good can come from a negative situation, the same way as unfavorable can come from a good problem.

Learn from your mistakes because remaining focused on the problem as a problem won't fix them. Evaluating the error to see what you can learn helps you move forward. As a Power Producer, it is up to you to continue to look at your situation and figure out how you can make an impact. When you are faced with rejection or failure, ask yourself: What can I learn from this? And then take the time to respond.

Reflection

If you have explored several areas and are still not sure how you bring value, you may need to dig a little deeper before you can choose which way you can be most useful in the value that you bring. Try answering these questions to get you started:

1. Which activities in my life get me the most excited?

2. Are there some things that excite me so much that they leave me energized and encouraged even days or weeks after?

When it comes to facing obstacles:

3. What are some current barriers that I am facing as a Power Producer?

4. How can I address those obstacles?

5. If I cannot address them, what are my reasons for not being able to address them?

6. If I can address them, what are some ways that I can overcome those obstacles?

CHAPTER EIGHT
EMBRACE
FOR IMPACT

The connection between people and the food chain can guide our understanding that lower status has no reflection on potential. To make any organization or company run effectively, it requires Power Producers.

For many years, I felt that my career was the summation of my value and worth. I did not attain top level status, and because of that I felt I wasn't worth much. Amidst that, I felt my position put me a place to be unseen and unheard. I met other individuals with different but comparable experiences and from all the conversations I had there is a resounding denominator of being worth less and feeling unsuccessful because of a lack of popularity or prestige.

The bottom of the food chain may make a lower salary and have less authority; however, the status quo of positions equating to power is not relevant when you believe that you have value to offer. It's time to uproot the labels assigned to the lower levels and experience the respect society willingly gives to the top so that Power Producers can be nurtured and keep all ecosystems healthy and stable.

The challenge to appreciate the effort and contribute value, regardless of status, is nothing new. In historical accounts renowned figures were supported by lesser-known individuals. Work completed behind the scenes contributed heavily to the result witnessed and then remembered by many. Fast forward to today, and modern-day society is not much different. There are artists, philanthropists, and politicians that are not considered to be on the same level of success as those with higher visibility. However, there is still a critical role that each person plays to reach the end goal, so it is important to emphasize that lower status does not minimize worth.

People "at the bottom" need to know how invaluable they are because irrespective of the role, everyone has greatness to offer. Any business and its operations demonstrate that the most significant strength is found in its employees, and if their contribution ceases to exist, every stakeholder will feel the impact. Maintaining a healthy food chain and energy pyramid starting from the bottom creates pride, retention, and productivity, and that is always important for business.

From the stories, examples, and research shared in these last chapters, you can see where the *real* power resides. And suppose you have found yourself resonating with what was shared. In that case, I think you are ready to assume the crucial role you play in your community and company. If you embrace the role of a Power Producer and then sustain and grow, you can bring an immense contribution. But before you're off impacting food chains for the better, I want to offer some last words of encouragement.

It can be disheartening to see your work glossed over, especially when every push of effort took more energy than you could muster. But I want to encourage you that your position has no bearing on your capabilities. Your level of knowledge and status has no bearing on your power, strength, or self-worth. When we only focus on one level, or only on salary, or only on one thing, we lose focus. As a Power Producer, there are many great things that you possess, and what you decide to do with those is up to *you*.

The potential of the bottom of the food chain for years we have seen as a place of limited possibilities. And while it isn't the top, there is much to be said for the power at the bottom. For years I struggled to believe this about myself, and if I'm honest, I occasionally still have struggles. But then I remember that every action has an impact. I think about all the effects of life. I can't remember the exact words for every moment. I can't remember the precise locations of the change. But I can remember that feeling. I can remember that so many people have poured into me. I remember that I have my ecosystem of supporters. People who have supported me at every level of my journey. People whose actions have planted a tiny seed that grew inside me. Other people who have nurtured me, challenges that tested me, and with time— have grown me into the person I am today. And the same is for you, so embrace *your* power. The bottom of the food chain isn't a bad place to be. It's a start to building confidence, gaining respect, and making an impact.

Being at the bottom of the food chain doesn't have to be your career or end goal. But whether it is or isn't, being at the bottom of the food chain allows you to embrace something usually seen as unfavorable. If your goal is to be a head chef and you are currently in the dish washer position, you are doing great. Don't take that position for granted. Don't discount what you do. Find a way to make that position work. Create impact with that position.

All food chain and energy pyramid levels are essential. Yet, much of what we see in books, television, marketing, and other media is devoted to reaching the top. Sometimes even when you give your best, you may still not be considered at the top of the game, which can be hard to accept. But, the world needs Power Producers. You may not be at the forefront of minds, but you are at the forefront of change, so commend yourself for where you are, acknowledge your assiduous efforts thus far. Recognize that success comes in different ways.

Being at the bottom of the food chain doesn't mean you can't make a change. You are worthy and it's your choice to make. Here are two final questions to reflect on.

Final Reflection

1. When will I start?

2. Do I want more information on becoming a Power Producer for my organization (eco-system) or how to create an organization that recognizes Power Producers?

If you answered yes, visit:
www.laporalindsey.com for more information.

THE FOOD CHAIN

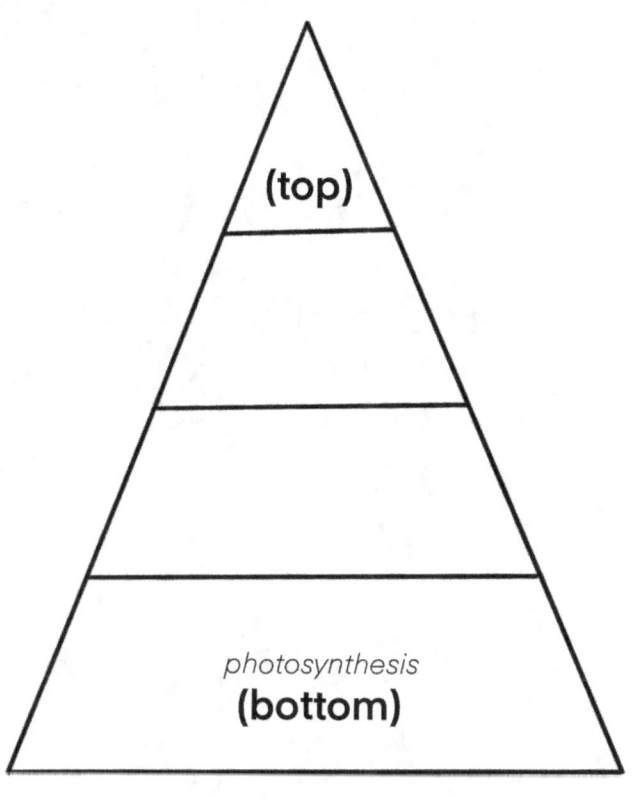

(top)

photosynthesis
(bottom)

ABOUT THE BOOK

xi   **ACKNOWLEDGEMENTS**

xii   **ABOUT THE AUTHOR**

Acknowledgements

Thank you to those who supported the making
of this book:
Editor:
Brunella Costagliola at The Military Editor Agency
Cover and Interior Design: Dee the Creative
Illustrator: Kristen Ritter

Thank you to my friends and family who believed in me.
From the moment I said I would start this project and
share this story, you said you would support me, and you
have. Words cannot express how grateful I am of your
support throughout this time.

And finally, a special thanks to my family. To my kids,
Naomi and James thank you for always asking, "Is your
book done yet?" Your curiosity was a nice reminder that
I must finish what I started. I love you both.

To my husband, Jesse, you supported me with your love
and understanding. I endeavored to do something with
absolutely no plan on how to do it. Even when I made
some costly mistakes as I tried to figure this all out, you
simply looked at me and said, "I love you," and for all of
that and more, "I love you too."

About the Author

LaPora's specialty is making a positive impact in low visibility roles. She has spent most of her career in positions where her actions were not witnessed, but they were still essential to the success of the organization and her community.

As an inspirational speaker, career coach, and writer, LaPora helps others understand that opportunities are created when the focus is on self-development and not titles. All impact is not visible or upfront, so even if you aren't "in charge," you still hold power.

LaPora credits life lessons from her professional and personal experience to her ability to deliver inspirational keynotes and develop workshops that allow

LaPora Lindsey
SPEAKER • COACH • AUTHOR

others to build a career and make an impact, no matter their position or title.

As a military spouse and avid volunteer, LaPora enjoys working with organizations that emphasize career development, advocacy, and inclusion for job seekers of all ages. When she is not working, she enjoys dancing and playing board games with her husband and children.

Visit website for more information:
www.laporalindsey.com